The Partition of Africa
1880–1900

LANCASTER PAMPHLETS

The Partition of Africa
1880–1900

and European Imperialism
in the Nineteenth Century

John M. MacKenzie

METHUEN · LONDON AND NEW YORK

First published in 1983 by
Methuen & Co. Ltd
11 New Fetter Lane,
London EC4P 4EE

Published in the USA by
Methuen & Co.
in association with Methuen, Inc.
733 Third Avenue, New York,
NY 10017

Typeset in Great Britain by
Scarborough Typesetting Services
and printed by
Richard Clay (The Chaucer Press)
Bungay, Suffolk

British Library Cataloguing in
Publication Data

MacKenzie, J. M.
The partition of Africa
– (Lancaster pamphlets)
1. Africa – Colonization – History
2. Africa – History – 19th century
I. Title   II. Series
960' .2   DT31
ISBN 0–416–35050–X

Foreword

Lancaster Pamphlets offer concise and up-to-date accounts of major historical topics, primarily for the help of students preparing for Advanced Level examinations, though they should also be of value to those pursuing introductory courses in universities and other institutions of higher education. They do not rely upon prior textbook knowledge. Without being all-embracing, their aims are to bring some of the central themes or problems confronting students and teachers into sharper focus than the textbook writer can hope to do; to provide the reader with some of the results of recent research which the textbook may not embody; and to stimulate thought about the whole interpretation of the topic under discussion. They are written by experienced university scholars who have a strong interest in teaching as well as an expertise, based on their own research, in the subject concerned.

Time-chart

Before 1870

1815	British acquisition of Cape from Dutch
1830	French acquisition of Algeria
	Discovery of mouths of Niger
1835	Great Trek of the Boers from Cape Colony
1849	Appointment of British Consul of Bights of Benin and Biafra
1852	Start of British steamship service to west Africa
1854	First successful Niger expedition using quinine as a prophylactic
1861	British annexation of Lagos
1863	French annexation of Porto Novo, later abandoned as result of mistake
1864	Ashanti War in Gold Coast
1865	Select Committee of House of Commons on west Africa
1869	Discovery of diamonds beyond the Cape frontier, later Kimberley
	Opening of Suez Canal

1870s

1872	'Responsible government' for Cape
	Start of British steamship service to east Africa
1873	Death of Livingstone

	Appointment of Sir John Kirk to be British consul-general at Zanzibar

Appointment of Sir John Kirk to be British consul-
general at Zanzibar

Ashanti War

1875   Purchase of Suez Canal shares by Disraeli

Foundation of Scottish missions in Nyasaland

1876   Leopold's Brussels conference

1877   Formation of Leopold's International Africa
Association

Publication of V. A. Cameron's *Across Africa*

Mackinnon's scheme for east Africa

Foundation of missions in Uganda

British annexation of Transvaal

1878   Congress of Berlin. Britain acquires Cyprus, and
gives France free hand in Tunisia

Foundation of African Lakes Company

1879   Goldie creates the United Africa Company

Ambitious French scheme for railway to connect
Algeria to western Sudan

British defeated by Zulu

1880s

1880   German companies established in Cameroons

De Brazza's Makoko treaties accepted by French
Government in 1882.

1881   French invasion of Tunisia

Battle of Majuba Hill. British abandon efforts to
federate South Africa

1882   British invasion of Egypt

Goldie's company becomes National Africa Company

Stanley active in Congo, making treaties for
Leopold's association

Formation of Leopold's International Association for
the Congo

1883   French protectorate over Porto Novo

German merchant Lüderitz acquires harbour at Angra
Pequena

1884   Foundation of German Colonisation Society

Nachtigal in west Africa, Peters in east Africa
    collecting treaties for German colonization societies

Anglo-Portuguese treaty on Congo, not ratified

German protectorates over Cameroons, Togo and
    Angra Pequena

Acquisition of British Somaliland

1884–5	Conference of Berlin
1885	Treaty of Berlin
	Death of General Gordon
	British protectorate over Oil Rivers
	German protectorate in east Africa
	Colony and protectorate in Bechuanaland (British)
	Italians take Eritrea
	Foundation of German East Africa Company
1885–6	Discovery of gold in Transvaal
1886	Royal Niger Company chartered
	Boundary Commission in east Africa to demarcate British and German spheres
1888	Imperial British East Africa Company chartered
1889	British South Africa Company chartered
	Italian acquisition of Somaliland

1890s

1890	Rhodes's pioneer column to Rhodesia
	Anglo-German Heligoland treaty demarcating spheres in east and central Africa
1891	British protectorate in Nyasaland
1894	French conquest of Dahomey
	Winding up of Imperial British East Africa Company
1894–5	Protectorates over Kenya and Uganda
1895–6	Jameson Raid
	Ashanti War
1896	British expand Sierra Leone by addition of protectorate in hinterland
	British decision to build east African railway
	Italians defeated at Battle of Adowa
1896–8	Kitchener's campaign in the Sudan

1898	Anglo-French confrontation at Fashoda
1899	Winding up of Royal Niger Company. Formation of protectorates of northern and southern Nigeria
	Outbreak of Boer War

1900s

1900–1	Ashanti War
1902	End of Boer War
1904	Anglo-French colonial agreements
1905–6	Moroccan crisis and Algeciras conference
1910	Dominion status in South Africa
1911	Agadir/Morocco crisis
1912	Morocco partitioned by France and Spain
	Acquisition of Libya by Italy

The Partition of Africa 1880–1900

and European Imperialism
in the Nineteenth Century

We have been witnesses of one of the most remarkable episodes in the history of the world.

So wrote Sir John Scott Keltie in the opening sentence of his book *The Partition of Africa*, published in 1893. Keltie and his contemporaries were enthralled by the statistics of that 'most remarkable episode'. More than 10 million square miles of African territory and over 100 million African people had fallen to European rule in the space of little more than a decade. The concluding acts of the Partition were yet to come in the late 1890s and in the years immediately preceding the first world war, but in Keltie's time the map of Africa was already beginning to look like its modern counterpart. In the middle of the century the European cartographer saw Africa as a continent of blank spaces where the principal physical features – rivers, lakes, mountains – were gradually being filled in by European exploration. In the late 1880s and early 1890s maps of Africa in school atlases were revised every year, for political boundaries and various colourings for the different empires were now the rage.

Since the publication of Keltie's book, writers and historians have conducted an energetic debate on the causes of the Partition of Africa, culminating in a veritable flood of books and articles in the last twenty years. This enduring interest is perhaps not surprising. The Scramble for Africa (as the Partition is sometimes more luridly known) was the most dramatic instance of the partition of the world by Europe and America in the late nineteenth century. It inaugurated a great revolution in the relationship between European and African peoples, and it sent out political, economic and social shock-waves, which continue to be felt in Africa to this day. Africans naturally find the Partition a distasteful event, yet they are prepared to defend the artificial boundaries established by it to the point of war if necessary. The modern challenge to Africa remains the struggle to consolidate and develop the national and economic units carved out by Europeans in the Partition period, and so knowledge of the Partition is fundamental to an understanding of contemporary Africa.

This pamphlet is concerned, however, with one great problem. What were the causes of the Partition of Africa and why did it occur when it did? Why was it that, after several centuries of nibbling at the edges of Africa, Europeans suddenly rushed in to establish direct military and political control over almost the entire continent? Why did European politicians who had traditionally resisted the extension of empire in Africa become caught up in a hectic demarcation of territory?

The actual events of the Partition and the explanations offered for it are highly complex. To boil them down into the short space of this pamphlet necessitates careful subdivision and the provision of signposts to help you through the maze of interpretations. The material that follows is divided into two main sections, Description and Interpretation. In the descriptive section, the historical background to the Partition will be sketched in, and then the actual events of the Scramble will be surveyed in the four main regions of Africa, north, west, south and east. In Section 2 each of the explanations offered for the Partition will be laid out, and that will be followed by an attempt at a conclusion based on recent thinking on the subject. There are, however, no final answers to such a complex problem. You must yourselves debate which of the interpretations of the causes of 'one of the most remarkable episodes in the history of the world' seems most convincing.

Historical background and the events of the Partition

At first sight it may seem surprising that Europeans did not successfully penetrate Africa until the late nineteenth century, for Africa is after all Europe's nearest neighbour, and the first continent with which Europe had established contact, both in the ancient world and at the beginning of the modern period. North Africa was a most important part of the Roman empire, as the great Roman remains of Libya, Tunisia and Algeria, as magnificent as any in Rome itself, testify. When Spain and Portugal began tentatively to explore south and west in the fifteenth century in their efforts to outflank the power of Islam in the Mediterranean, inevitably their first contacts were with Africa. Spain established a number of small colonial enclaves in north Africa which she holds to this day. In the sequence of voyages associated with the school of navigation of Prince Henry the Navigator the Portuguese felt their way round the African Atlantic coast, established themselves on offshore islands and at one or two points on the mainland, all this before Columbus set out on his epic voyage for the Americas.

Africa has sometimes been depicted as no more than a giant barrier to the real objective of Europeans in the fifteenth, sixteenth and seventeenth centuries, Asia. But Africa was a vital part of the Portuguese design. For many centuries African gold – from the region of the modern country of Ghana – had appeared in north Africa, brought by the Moors across the caravan routes of the Sahara. On the east coast, Muslims traded gold from Zimbabwe, sending it to the Middle East and India. The Portuguese wished to divert this trade into their own hands, for they needed gold to pay for the spices they sought in south India and elsewhere in the East.

One of the first Portuguese settlements on the west African coast was called, rather hopefully, El Mina, the mine. In east Africa they succeeded by the late sixteenth century in penetrating the Zambezi region and establishing settlements and trading posts on the highlands of the modern Zimbabwe. But these efforts to secure the African gold trade to themselves failed. Not only did they never actually reach the sources of the gold, their position was always a very weak one. In the course of the seventeenth

3

century they were subjected to constant revolts, and in the 1690s all their positions in the interior of south-central Africa were destroyed.

This helps us to understand why Europeans failed to penetrate Africa as successfully as they penetrated the Americas and Asia in this period. Africans successfully resisted them. It used to be customary to explain European difficulties in Africa in terms of geography, climate and disease. It is true that Africa has few navigable rivers; it is true that in the west Europeans on the coast were separated from the interior by forest, and in the south and east both by arid areas just inland from the coast and by the escarpment that forms the edge of the high plateau of east, central and southern Africa; it is also true that Europeans suffered high mortality rates through fevers, and, more importantly perhaps, found it impossible to use draught animals like the horse and the ox to penetrate Africa because none could survive the sickness borne by the tsetse fly. But Europeans in other continents faced very considerable difficulties which they were able to overcome. The forest in west Africa was in fact criss-crossed by trade routes, as was the Sahara Desert to the north. The Portuguese managed to hold trading posts in the interior of the Zambezi region for over 70 years, despite problems of disease and terrain. But at this stage Europe did not enjoy the military preponderance she was to establish later. Just beyond the coastal belt of west Africa lay a sequence of powerful states, many of them with well-organized armies. There were important states in east and central Africa also, and a black military revolution in southern Africa in the early nineteenth century provided some African peoples with fresh powers of resistance there too. Europeans continued to be defeated by Africans, for example the Ashanti, the Zulu and the Abyssinians, until the late nineteenth century.

Despite repeated failures, however, Europeans continued to cling to the coasts of Africa. In the course of the seventeenth century, the Portuguese had been joined by the Dutch, the English, the French, the Danes, and traders from the north German ports. They established fortified trading posts at various places on the west African coast. They would have liked to reach the sources of gold and other commodities they wished to trade

4

from Africa, but they had no need to do so. African middlemen successfully supplied the European coastal positions for more than 200 years. This was particularly true of the slave trade. Europeans created a great demand in the American colonies, the Caribbean and South America. Africans supplied that demand, and European merchants and shipping interests made large profits from it. Africa had now fulfilled two auxiliary roles in the European scheme – first as the supplier of gold to pay for the Asian trade, next as the supplier of slaves for the plantations, cotton, tobacco and sugar of the Americas.

For the most part, Europeans hoped that they would make only brief trading visits to Africa, for the death rates of the west coast were certainly extremely high. However, Europeans did succeed in settling in a few places. Spaniards settled in Morocco. Portuguese settled in the Zambezi Valley, but there they inter-married with the local population and soon ceased to be fully European. Only at the Cape did Europeans settle successfully and maintain their racial exclusiveness. The Dutch established a 'refreshment station' at the Cape of Good Hope in 1652 to supply their ships sailing to the Indies. Soon grants of land for permanent settlement were being made, and the Dutch began an expansion into the interior that was to have incalculable consequences in later centuries.

During the first half of the nineteenth century it became apparent that significant changes in the pattern of Europe's relationship with Africa were on the way. Africa was beginning to be important for the commodities it could supply directly to Europe, most notably palm oil and groundnuts from west Africa, ivory and other products, including a plantation-grown spice called cloves, from east Africa. In west Africa Europeans were beginning to understand more about the interior. The Senegal and Gambia rivers had become important arteries of trade. The route of the Niger and the fact that the 'Oil Rivers' were its delta had been established by 1830. By the middle of the century, the effectiveness of a medicine, quinine, to ward off malaria was well attested and Europeans were able to survive in west and other parts of Africa. In southern Africa the slow advance of Europeans into the interior quickened dramatically in the 1830s when parties

5

of Dutch farmers (also known as Afrikaners or Boers) decided to escape the irksome characteristics – as they saw them – of British rule (established when the British took the Cape from the Dutch during the Napoleonic Wars) by seeking new lands on the relatively healthy uplands further from the coast. In east Africa, more and more traders were anxious to exploit a growing trade – Indians from the west of India, Americans, French, British and Germans.

The middle of the century was the era of the explorers. These explorers were a new breed, individualists who explored for a variety of different purposes. Some were missionaries who prospected Africa for Christian opportunity; others were geographers, naturalists, journalists or propagandists for imperial expansion. Most of them were linked to the geographical societies of their home countries. Since the late eighteenth century, geographical knowledge had been seen, together with related botanical and mineralogical knowledge, as crucial to Europe's discovery and exploitation of man's global environment. Explorers were well aware of the practical application of their discoveries, and most of them became highly successful publicists. Many of them found fame and fortune, for their works became best-sellers. By the 1870s and 1880s, the explorers were taking on a new significance. Now their activities became directly connected with the spread of European power. They moved faster, less concerned with precise geographical and natural observation, more concerned to prospect Africa for potential annexation. Their work was nationalistic, concerned to thwart the activities of other European explorers in a developing scramble for possession. Yet all these strands had already come together in the work of the most remarkable of them, David Livingstone. He was a distinguished and observant scientist, but his science was devoted to the spread of Christianity and commerce (his own phrase for what he saw as a two-pronged civilizing mission), white settlement and European power. He died in 1873, before the Scramble for Africa had really begun, but his speeches and his books, together with the individuals whom he influenced, were to have a very considerable effect on the future.

By 1880, the eve of the Partition, the European penetration of

Africa and the Ottoman Empire c. 1870

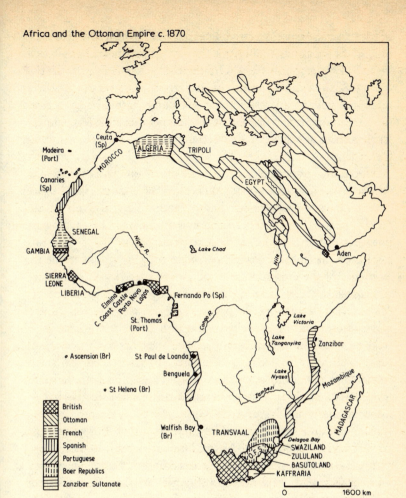

Madeira (Port)

Ceuta (Sp)

Canaries (Sp)

MOROCCO

ALGERIA

TRIPOLI

EGYPT

Aden

SENEGAL

Niger R.

Lake Chad

Nile

GAMBIA

SIERRA LEONE

LIBERIA

Elmina
C. Coast Castle
Porto Novo
Lagos

Fernando Po (Sp)

Congo R.

St. Thomas (Port)

Lake Victoria

Lake Tanganyika

Zanzibar

Ascension (Br)

St Paul de Loanda

Benguela

Lake Nyasa

Mozambique

St Helena (Br)

Zambezi

MADAGASCAR

British
Ottoman
French
Spanish
Portuguese
Boer Republics
Zanzibar Sultanate

Walfish Bay (Br)

TRANSVAAL

Delagoa Bay

SWAZILAND

O.F.S.

ZULULAND

BASUTOLAND

KAFFRARIA

0   1600 km

7

Africa and of African states and peoples had taken a variety of new forms. Some rulers, mainly in the north, had fallen deeply into debt to European creditors. Others had become a prey to concession-seekers, who sought concessions to build railway lines, harbours, telegraph systems, and to conduct trade. Many African rulers had decided to use Europeans to introduce modern administrative or military methods to their states and perhaps help them to establish power over their neighbours. This was true, for example, in Egypt and in the east African Sultanate of Zanzibar. Chiefs and kings in west, south and east Africa attempted to use missionaries as informal advisers and allies. Travellers and explorers in Africa now invariably carried a bag of treaty forms, whereby they persuaded African rulers to accept the 'protection' of European states. Most chiefs were only dimly aware of the contents of these treaties – which were indeed sometimes mistranslated to them – and in any case many failed to appreciate the power these travelling Europeans represented. After all, Europeans did not arrive in trains or even on horseback. Mostly they walked, and travelled in no more state than African rulers themselves. Only on the coast and on river banks was the power of steam apparent as more and more steam vessels appeared, sailed up the rivers, and were even dismantled and carried overland to be used on the inland lakes.

Everywhere, in short, an advance guard of Europeans was appearing in the interior of Africa. No longer did they merely pass through the land, as explorers, prospectors and hunters had done. Now more permanent stations and settlements appeared. Trading posts were set up on the rivers in the interior of west Africa; mission stations were constructed well inland in west, east and southern Africa. Boer settlers, always searching for vast farms (3000 hectares and more) on which to run their cattle, were thinking of moving across the River Limpopo into central Africa.

But so far European countries had seldom been prepared to extend their political authority to cover these inland positions. Traders, missionaries and settlers operated beyond the limits of European or colonial power. They fended for themselves, carved out their own domains, established their own law. To use a word common in today's international power-play, all of these elements were destabilizing traditional states in Africa, disrupting the trading balance, with its moderate ends and limited means, which had existed earlier in the century.

Until the 1880s, European powers had shown little interest in extending their 'formal' power in Africa because to do so seemed like a costly and unnecessary arrangement. Trade, which constituted only a tiny fraction of world trade, was conducted with reasonable continuity, although in some places disruptions did seem to be on the increase. Where real crises occurred, 'informal' influence could be exerted. Advisers could be moved in, financial arrangements made for the payment of debts, consuls appointed to protect European nationals, and commercial treaties signed. It seemed that, so long as merchants could maintain the 'open door' for their trade, they were uninterested in control by governments, which often meant the extension of costly customs dues.

Why did all this change? Why did European merchants and others press for protection by their home governments, and why did those governments suddenly see virtue in establishing 'formal' rule in Africa? To answer this question we need to examine the new developments taking place in each of the main regions of Africa.

NORTH AFRICA

North Africa has always looked two ways. It was both part of the Mediterranean world and also part of greater Africa, united to the former by long-standing commercial networks and by the imperial ambitions of Rome, the Arabs and the Ottoman Turks, yet linked to Africa by the great trading routes of the Sahara in the west and by the Nile system in the east. By the nineteenth century, a number of factors had come to influence the European approach to north Africa. First, Napoleon's great expedition to Egypt in 1798 had made the British all the more aware of the significance of north Africa to the routes to India which already utilized the land bridges of the isthmus of Suez and the Levant (connecting to the great Mesopotamian river systems and the Gulf). It was these considerations that led the British to acquire Malta in 1800 as an important strategic point dominating the north African coast and offering a refreshment station between Gibraltar and the eastern Mediterranean. Second, the links of suzerainty within the Ottoman empire were beginning to loosen at this period. Although in theory the Ottoman empire at Constantinople continued to receive the allegiance of all the rulers of north Africa, they were in fact beginning to emerge as independent potentates. Mehemet Ali, the great ruler in Egypt in the early nineteenth century, led the way in this. He developed his own imperial pretensions, and began to establish his own commercial and financial links with Europeans. Other North African rulers were to follow suit, and in doing so raised the dangerous spectre of European involvement in their states. Third, Europeans developed ambitions to turn their respective areas of the Mediterranean into exclusive spheres of commercial and political influence. Spain had failed to assert herself over the north African coast in rolling back the Moors, but she had retained her small enclaves there. The French and the Italians were to attempt to turn first the western Mediterranean and then the central Mediterranean into respectively French and Italian lakes.

The French began the process in 1830 when, during the dying weeks of the old Bourbon monarchy, they annexed Algeria. From the 1850s they began to develop ideas of a great western African French dominion, extending from the Mediterranean to the west African coast, but it was not until the 1870s, when these ideas came to be coupled with grandiose trans-Saharan railway schemes, that they began to find favour with French politicians. By then, the partition of North Africa had become even more closely bound up with the decline of the Ottoman empire. A crucial turning-point was the crisis of 1877–8, when the western European powers attempted to frustrate Russian designs on Ottoman territory, but in doing so they themselves ate into Ottoman power. The British acquired the island of Cyprus to complement Gibraltar and Malta in their system of strategic posts in the Mediterranean. In return for French acceptance of this, the British agreed to give the French a free hand in Tunisia. The French waited until 1881 before cashing in this diplomatic cheque. On the pretext of punishing cross-border raiders into Algeria, they took Tunis and its hinterland, despite – or perhaps

10

because of – the presence of many Italian merchants and matching Italian ambitions there.

Some have argued that the Partition really begins in 1869 with the opening of the Suez Canal, or at least in 1875 when Disraeli acquired the Khedive's Suez Canal shares (seven-sixteenths of the whole) for Britain. The Canal made the strategic significance of Egypt, recognized by Napoleon, all the more apparent. Within a few years of the Canal's opening, 80 per cent of all the ships passing through were British, yet the Canal had been built by French capital and seemed to be dominated by France until the British capitalized on the financial difficulties of the Egyptian ruler by buying his shares. Since Mehemet Ali, successive rulers of Egypt had attempted to turn Egypt into a modern state. This had, however, led them into increasing financial difficulties since projects had not always been well thought out, and Egyptian revenue could not adequately cover the huge burden of interest payments on the debts incurred. Although Europeans had added to these problems by the manner in which the loans had been arranged, they became alarmed at the instability of the Egyptian financial and political systems. The bondholders who had made the loans were disturbed about the prospect of Egyptian bankruptcy and the repudiation of debt, and governments, particularly the British, were afraid that the Canal might fall into the hands of those who might wish to exploit their command of the jugular vein of the Oriental trade. This led the British and the French to set up financial commissions to examine the state of the Egyptian debt, and eventually to create a joint supervision of Egyptian finances from 1878.

By 1882, these arrangements had produced opposition in Egypt because they seemed to detract from Egyptian independence. A nationalist movement, led by a young army officer called Colonel Arabi, seemed likely to capture the Egyptian government. The British decided to intervene. After a riot in Alexandria in which fifty Europeans were killed, the Royal Navy bombarded the city, a large military force was landed, and the movement led by Colonel Arabi was crushed. The British now found themselves supervising the Egyptian government. They did not take formal control of Egypt until the outbreak of the first world war, and on

11

many occasions after 1882 they protested that they were about to depart, but they had become the *de facto* rulers of the country. The British Government would have preferred it if the French had joined them in their invasion and in the extended supervision of Egypt, but domestic problems in France precluded French involvement. The French resented the new British power in Egypt, and it has been suggested that it was this resentment which helped to develop the pace of the partition in west Africa and elsewhere (see Section 2).

Involvement in Egypt did, however, lead to the British involvement in the entire Nile region. The death in 1885 of General Gordon, who was administering the Sudan for Egypt, led to one of the greatest public outcries of the age. Gordon became an imperial martyr and a source of Christian resentment against the Islamic forces that had led to this European reverse. Yet it was not until the late 1890s that the British, now again fearing French ambitions in a horizontal line across Africa from the western Sudan to the Nile, set about avenging the loss of Gordon. Between 1896 and 1898 Kitchener reconquered the Sudan, and destroyed French designs there. By now the British were in command of the source and upper reaches of the White Nile in Uganda. After a French expedition to the Nile under Colonel Marchand had reached Fashoda in 1898, where they encountered Kitchener's forces, the British Government used an ultimatum to warn France off the region. The entire White Nile system was British in one form or another, and this proved to be the last source of Anglo-French tension.

By 1898 the whole of sub-Saharan Africa had been partitioned, with the exception of Liberia and Ethiopia. But the partition of north Africa was not yet complete. When the British and French sealed their entente in 1904, they agreed on colonial arrangements that would give the French a free hand in Morocco. But the French did not act on this until German ambitions there seemed to threaten their position. Even so, it was not until there had been two Moroccan crises that Morocco was partitioned between France and Spain in 1912. Italian ambitions were at last satisfied with their acquisition of Libya, also in 1912.

Since the sixteenth and seventeenth centuries Europeans had traded on the west African coast, using fortified 'factories' as their bases. By the early nineteenth century some of these had developed into embryo colonies. The British had founded a settlement at Freetown, Sierra Leone, in the 1780s, where they could land freed slaves. They also had possessions at the mouth of the Gambia River and on the Gold Coast. The main area of French interest was on the Senegal River and its adjacent coast, where the French actually attempted a settlement of Europeans from 1818. This failed. From the 1840s they had established themselves in several positions on the Ivory Coast. In 1849 the British appointed a consul for the Bights of Benin and Biafra, thereby making a preliminary claim to a sphere of influence in the Niger region. In addition to the significant spheres of influence of the French and the British, there were trading settlements and forts belonging to the Portuguese, the Spanish, the Dutch, the Danes, the German Hanseatic ports and Brandenburg. Thus, amid a complicated patchwork of European positions, certain areas of specific interest had been carved out, and these tended to be emphasized as the century progressed.

To make the situation even more complex, the merchants of each country did not necessarily operate from their national bases. Indeed, they very often avoided doing so, precisely to evade paying customs dues, such duties being levied at the forts and small colonies in order to pay for protection and for the administration. The operations of merchants trading palm oil, groundnuts and other commodities set up complicated series of relationships with each other, with their respective national administrations, metropolitan and local, and with African traders and rulers. The very merchants who sought to avoid customs would demand protection when their trade or their installations seemed endangered. By the 1880s they were demanding the recognition of their particular areas of operation as spheres of national interest from which they could attempt to cut out rivals from other nationalities.

All of this created a very fluid situation on the West African coast. Gradual French and British advances took place, which officials in the Foreign Office in London described as 'creeping imperialism'. There were a number of reasons for these extensions of territory. One was the repeated involvement of 'men on the spot', administrators of the various forts and colonies, in areas beyond their strict jurisdiction. They often became concerned that merchants were avoiding customs dues by the simple expedient of landing at a spot further along the coast. This undermined the financial viability of their own administrations, and it was a powerful argument to put to London or Paris that a sideways extension of territory would increase revenue, and make their small colonies more self-sufficient. Another was concern for the 'turbulent frontier'. Wars between African peoples, often for the control of the very trade routes which fed the coastal territories, could disrupt trade, and then governors and administrators would be under great pressure to intervene. They repeatedly argued to London or Paris that an extension of territory into the hinterland would lead to the suppression of strife and the consequent freeing of trade routes.

There were two other reasons for the extension of territory. Europeans in west Africa, like Europeans everywhere in the world since the expansion of Europe from the fifteenth century, tended to become involved in local politics. They often attempted to increase their influence by establishing relationships with rulers who would best serve their interests. Some administrators in west Africa paid stipends to African chiefs beyond their territorial frontiers to keep them 'sweet'. Rulers might be supported against rivals; insurgents might be helped against an established hostile ruler. Often, the Europeans were themselves used in the astute diplomacy of African kings and chiefs. Finally, traders, governors and administrators tended to react aggressively if they imagined that a rival power was about to establish a sphere of influence in an area that they regarded as impinging on their own commercial region. When this occurred, the Foreign Offices in London and Paris found it difficult to disavow the actions of their subordinates because of the serious loss of face involved in appearing to give in to a rival power.

All these pressures were building up in the decades before the Scramble, and several extensions of territory took place. The

1860s were, however, years that reflected the ambivalence of the British about the whole process. On the one hand, in 1861, they annexed Lagos, a principality (now the capital of modern Nigeria) where they had meddled in the succession in the past, and which was important because it dominated the entrance to a long navigable creek which gave access to an important stretch of coast. They did so because they thought the ruler was still involved in the slave trade, and because the strategic position of the town gave him an undue opportunity to disrupt trade. Britain's possession of Lagos was to lead to considerable complications, rivalries with the French, involvement in the politics of the Yoruba people beyond the coast (where missionaries were already well established), and so on. It was a classic instance of the manner in which 'creeping imperialism' begat imperialism. Yet in 1865, a Select Committee of the House of Commons produced a report suggesting that there should be no further extensions of British rule in west Africa, and that efforts should be made to withdraw from some of the existing commitments on the coast. That Committee has often been used by historians as evidence of anti-imperial sentiment at the time, but it met in the wake of a disastrous campaign against the Ashanti in 1864, and it is now apparent that it was packed with a particular group of anti-imperial Members of Parliament. In reality, the policy of restraining advance proved unworkable. For a number of years, the British Foreign Office attempted to exercise that policy, but on the west African coast rivalries and tensions prompted further small extensions of territory.

The French tended to be less ambivalent. On various occasions they attempted to push their influence deeper into the interior of their Senegal colonies, but they found themselves checked by powerful Muslim sultanates. This contributed to their developing belief that Islamic power had to be broken by French military might if their conception of economic development were to be put into practice. Advances were made in the 1850s and again in the late 1870s, associated with the governors Faidherbe and Brière de L'Isle. Such concerns were at first more related to developments in French domestic politics than they were to the pressures of French mercantile activity. In the 1850s, the newly established

15

Second Empire of Napoleon III required a territorial extension to justify its imperial pretensions. By the late 1870s the French were attempting to lick the wounds to national pride caused by the Franco-Prussian War and the loss of the provinces of Alsace-Lorraine. From this time, two important parties vied with each other on the French political scene, a colonial party that sought to provide France with a great empire to match her historical claims, and an Alsace-Lorraine party which regarded all overseas activity as a diversion from the real end of securing revenge against Germany and the restoration of the lost provinces. The French Government was soon also subjected to the mercantile pressures emanating from the great ports of Bordeaux and Marseilles, anxious to ensure that French commercial spheres in west Africa were not lost. Individual traders, like the rich and influential Victor Régis, secured French consulships for themselves and their employees, and took a hand in pressing forward small acts of annexation to secure their trade. As the period progressed, the merchants found Paris more receptive and pressure groups more assiduous in their support. By 1879 the French had begun to develop a visionary notion of a vast west African empire linking Algeria to the western Sudan, consolidated by the building of a great trans-Saharan railway.

No such visions animated the British Government, but there was a similar interaction between the pressures of local west African merchants and the activities of interest groups in Britain, like the chambers of commerce of several British cities. There were no major British withdrawals. They continued to attempt to stop up breaches in their commercial system to prevent the drain of customs dues. They continued to be pulled inland by turbulence in the hinterland. In 1879, for example, the number of trading caravans reaching Sierra Leone dropped by four-fifths as a result of inland warfare. There could be no stronger argument for interior annexation, since such a collapse in trade also seriously damaged the administration's revenues. Moreover, the tensions between Britain and France were exacerbated by new opportunities to dominate the trade of entire regions. The Danes had sold their forts to the British in 1850, and the Dutch also gave up their possession in 1872. These larger spheres gave rise to growing

16

anxieties that whole areas would be cut off from trade by a protectionist rival. French efforts to drive deeper into the interior of west Africa raised alarm among British commercial interests who sought to confirm the vague British claim to dominate the Niger region. In 1879, a British businessman, George Goldie, alarmed by what he saw as the aggressive expansion of French competition, succeeded in uniting all the British interests on the Niger into one company, the United Africa Company. From that time, this company was dedicated to the exclusion of the French from its sphere, and the confirmation of British power over the entire length of the navigable Niger. Eventually, the company became the main vehicle of British imperialism in the Niger region through its acquisition in 1886 of a charter to trade and to govern there.

Just as these Anglo-French tensions were building to a climax, two new maverick elements seemed to galvanize the 'creeping' partition of west Africa. A European monarch, King Leopold of the Belgians, had for some time harboured ambitions to establish for himself a great private colony, either in Asia or in Africa. He was enthralled by the remarkable story of the British Brooke family, who had become the Rajahs of Sarawak on the far eastern island of Borneo. In the 1870s his attention was drawn to the west-central region of Africa by the writings of the naval officer and explorer Verney Lovett Cameron, and the journalist H. M. Stanley. In 1876 he called a conference of geographers and others interested in Africa in Brussels and set up the International Africa Association, a body supposedly dedicated to the humanitarian development of Africa. By the early 1880s he had agents collecting treaties from African chiefs in the Congo area. In 1880, a French explorer, de Brazza, had attempted to approach the Congo from the French territory of Gabon and had also made treaties, which were accepted by the French Government in 1882. British traders had developed interests in the Congo and were thoroughly alarmed at this activity. To counteract the claims of the French and of Leopold, the British decided to support Portuguese historic claims to control the mouth of the Congo, but British trading interests disliked the Portuguese, and the treaty negotiated between 1882 and 1884 was not ratified.

Leopold's ambitions had stimulated a struggle for control of the River Congo, which in three navigable stretches, separated by cataracts, provided access to a vast region of central Africa. His designs seemed to span Africa. He talked of a coastal outlet in east Africa, and even of reaching the Zambezi. Leopold's idea of a vast central African state therefore fomented scrambling anxieties in all three regions of sub-Saharan Africa.

The second maverick element appeared further north and west. In 1880 two German companies had established themselves in the Cameroons just east of the Niger delta. In 1884 a German explorer, Gustav Nachtigal, arrived there and proceeded to collect treaties from African chiefs. Nachtigal just beat the British consul Hewett, who had intended collecting treaties in the Cameroons himself, but was delayed by the necessity of establishing claims to the more important Oil Rivers, while the United Africa Company was busy treaty-making up the Niger. The British Government had in fact decided to take the Cameroons some time earlier, but the decision was held up in the trammels of Foreign Office bureaucracy for several months.

Bismarck had long declared himself to be opposed to the acquisition of colonies, but in 1884 he submitted to the colonial pressure groups by announcing protectorates in west and south-west Africa. Now heavily involved himself, he called a conference in Berlin in December 1884 to try to bring some order to the proceedings. The treaty produced by this international conference internationalized the Congo (an arrangement which soon became a dead letter), recognized the British sphere in the Niger, and laid down groundrules for further scrambling. Powers had to prove 'effective occupation' and inform their rivals before annexing territory. The treaty did little to bring order to the Partition; indeed it merely exacerbated it. The process of African treaty-making developed at an even faster pace. In a rapid sequence of developments into the 1890s, commercial coastal spheres were turned into inland colonies, African states were conquered, and boundary negotiations effected. The dates of these events can be studied in the time-chart at the beginning of the pamphlet.

SOUTHERN AND CENTRAL AFRICA

When we turn to southern Africa, we find again that a creeping

18

partition had been going on before the 1880s. For much of the century, the competition for land and resources in the interior of Africa had been developing in intensity. There was a number of parties to this competition, both white and black. The Boers had sought to satisfy their perpetual land hunger by constantly leap-frogging into the interior. In the late 1830s, this had taken an organized and particularly dramatic form when large parties had left British-controlled territory for the interior. The British had found it difficult to decide whether they should control this process or leave the Boers to their own devices. Of one thing they were sure, however, and that was that they had to control the coastline of southern Africa in order to protect their routes to the Indian Ocean and to India. This was why they annexed Natal in 1843, an action which sent many of the Boers who had settled there back over the Drakensberg Mountains into the interior.

White advance meant black contraction. A battle for resources among black people had been intensified when whites had cut off their opportunities for further southern expansion. In the early nineteenth century, a people known as the Zulu succeeded in creating a remarkable African state. That state was to make its name the most famous of all African peoples, certainly the one that impinged most strongly on the consciousness of the Victorians. They were to have a powerful effect on the partition of southern Africa in a number of ways.

The great internal conflicts of the Zulu state produced, in the 1820s and 1830s, waves of migration of disaffected groups which established new African states and often came to dominate local populations in the Transvaal, Zimbabwe, Mozambique, Malawi and Tanzania. These states were to prove vigorous in their efforts to resist white encroachment, although they also laid waste large areas that were to facilitate the white advance. Moreover, the depredations of the Zulus upon their neighbours caused some of them to draw together into 'defensive' states, states whose rulers were to become the most able of African diplomats of the nineteenth century. Their capacity to defend themselves, sharpened on the horns of the Zulu fighting system, led them later to attempt to save their states from the clutches of Boer settlers and European concessionaires, and to indulge in what has come to be known as

19

the 'scramble for protection'. By securing the support of missionaries, and by enlisting the aid of the humanitarian party in Britain, they sought to hand themselves over to what seemed to them to be the lesser evil of imperial rule. Such states included the Swazi, the Sotho under the great king Moshoeshoe, who added the good fortune of longevity to his other considerable capacities, and the Tswana under Khama, who perhaps most successfully of all manipulated missionaries and humanitarians.

The Zulus also fought a great war against the British. They achieved famous victories in 1879, but it was inevitable that they would go down in defeat once they had invoked the full wrath of their imperial opponents. When their state was defeated and broken, a vacuum was created which prompted further white advance; the removal of the Zulu threat helped to give the Boers new ambition for an expansive independence in the interior of Africa.

A dramatic new development was injected into this complex struggle for resources in the 1870s and 1880s. This has come to be known as the mineral revolution. In 1869 diamonds were discovered just beyond the frontier of the Cape Colony. Various peoples claimed the region, but the British soon annexed it under the pretext of bringing law and order to the diggings. It was shortly added to the area of the Cape Colony, and the economy of that colony was transformed. The diamond diggings at Kimberley inaugurated a revolution in a number of ways. They made the Cape Colony's economy self-sufficient enough to enable the British Government to grant responsible government (internal self-government) to it in 1872. This meant that there now existed in southern Africa a colonial agency which had its own expansionist ambitions independent of the imperial government. Second, capital flooded into southern Africa. Kimberley led directly to the creation of a fabulously wealthy local oligarchy, which would develop considerable territorial ambitions for itself. Its most famous member was Cecil Rhodes. The dramatic increase in the Cape Colony's trade provided the means for the development of railways and ports, which were to become a vital springboard for the further leap into the interior. The increased trade of southern Africa led to a considerable growth in shipping interests involved in the area, interests that were to constitute a most important pressure group at a later date.

The revolution moved into its second phase when gold in large quantities was discovered in the Boer Republic of the Transvaal in 1885–6. In 1877 the British had attempted to annex the Transvaal, but the Boers had resisted and the British had been defeated at the Battle of Majuba Hill in 1881. The British Liberal Government had declined to commit more troops and expend more money, but had allowed the Boers to regain their independence. They had done so in the belief that the Boer republics offered very little economic threat to the British colonies of the Cape and Natal, and were unlikely to interest outside powers. The discovery of gold changed all that. The Transvaal economy rushed ahead by leaps and bounds. Vast quantities of capital were attracted. The interest of foreign powers was aroused. The chances of Boer expansion to the coast were enhanced. Moreover, both diamonds and gold were to have incalculable effects on African society by creating a massive demand for black labour. Many African migrants acquired guns, and the whole process produced further disruptive effects on African peoples.

By the time gold was discovered in the Transvaal, the Scramble for southern Africa was already under way. German traders had begun to operate on the coast of south-west Africa, and at just the time that Nachtigal was active in west Africa these traders began to demand German protection. As in west Africa, the British fumbled, partly because the German threat was so unexpected, partly because the mills of the British governmental machine ground very slowly. The Germans declared a protectorate over Angra Pequena in south-west Africa in 1884, and now seemed likely to establish a claim in south-east Africa too. German concession seekers were active on a portion of coastline between the Cape and Natal which had not been annexed to either colony and also in a gap between Natal and the Portuguese possessions to the north. These areas would undoubtedly have been incorporated into the British colonies eventually, but the arrival of the Germans speeded up the process. The British Government for once moved quickly to separate the Germans from the Boers by securing the great wedge of Bechuanaland (Botswana) and the eastern coastal gaps. The Boers were now cut off from the sea and the Germans were prevented from encroaching on a British sphere.

Bechuanaland had an additional significance. For Rhodes it was 'the Suez Canal to the interior', a vital route to central Africa. The central African phase of the partition was largely pursued by local interests, Rhodes at their head. 'Cape imperialism' set out to thwart the Boers, the Germans, the Portuguese and King Leopold. The objectives were to destroy the historical claims of Portugal to a great belt of territory across Africa from Angola to Mozambique, to prevent the threatened Boer expansion north across the River Limpopo, to frustrate German efforts to approach central Africa from south-west Africa and from their new colony of Tanganyika in the east, to prevent Leopold from expanding his already vast Congo territory southwards, where there were known copper deposits, and to exploit once more the sources of gold in the interior. The medieval gold trade of east Africa had been based on Zimbabwe, and many thought that this was the biblical land of Ophir, King Solomon's mines. Acquiring this region would help Rhodes and his associates to redress the balance of power in southern Africa, overwhelm the Boers, and create an enlarged and federated southern Africa dominated by English-speakers.

Between 1888 and 1890 Rhodes manipulated in turn the local political situation at the Cape, the process of concession-hunting and treaty-making in the interior of Africa, his rivals in the hunt for concessions – who included the Boers, the Portuguese, envoys of King Leopold and some other British economic interests – and above all the Government of Lord Salisbury and influential sections of imperial opinion at home. He added political power to his considerable economic power by becoming premier of the Cape in 1890. His agents succeeded in securing vital concessions from the powerful King Lobengula of the Ndebele in Zimbabwe, and he bought out all his rivals and all opposition to him. He created a company, the British South Africa Company, which the British Government chartered to conduct its imperial work in central Africa, placing only very vague limitations on its operations, and even vaguer frontiers to its actual geographical sphere. Rhodes had successfully beaten back all rivals from the area that is

22

now Zambia and Zimbabwe. 'It was like being given Australia,' he enthused. He encouraged white settlement; he made war on African peoples; he even subsidized an imperial administration in Nyasaland (Malawi) to keep it alive against Portuguese threats; and he gave money to missionaries to develop education so that an African élite could be created to act as auxiliaries in his colonies.

As imperial attitudes in Britain developed, so did Rhodes's ambitions grow. He wished to create a vast dominion in southern and central Africa which would compare with Canada or Australia. To do this he had to reverse the events of 1881 and subvert the Boer republics once more. In the 1890s, he and his associates plotted with mine-owners and English-speaking workers in Johannesburg to overthrow the Transvaal Republic of Paul Kruger, now showing dangerous tendencies of forming an alliance with Germany. In 1895–6 Rhodes's effort to overthrow President Kruger failed miserably. The expected revolt in Johannesburg did not happen and what was supposed to be a revolution is known to history merely as the Jameson Raid. Rhodes fell from power, but eventually the imperial government, for reasons that are much too complex to examine here, and which have themselves been the subject of a considerable debate, accomplished some of his objectives in the Boer War of 1899–1902.

EAST AFRICA

In southern Africa, Britain was prepared to permit local colonial interests to act as agents in the imperial real estate game, agents who themselves often called the tune. In east Africa, the British had also established a relationship with an agency through which they hoped to achieve their economic and strategic ends. This was an agency of a very different sort, a remarkable trans-oceanic Muslim state. In the seventeenth century, the Portuguese had discovered that their most formidable foe was a small seafaring state in the Gulf of Oman, the Sultanate at Muscat. This Sultanate not only destroyed Portuguese efforts to dominate the Gulf, it also defeated the Portuguese in east Africa, removing them from Mombasa in 1698 and restricting them to Mozambique. The Omanis then attempted to establish command of the east African coastal trade for themselves. In the early nineteenth century a new ruler called Seyyid Said established his overlordship over almost all the coastal commercial towns of east Africa and created an important economic and naval base for himself on the island of Zanzibar. There he encouraged the development of what was in effect a whole new economic system. On the one hand, Zanzibar sought to tap the trade of the interior of east Africa and act as the entrepôt through which the trade would pass and be taxed in the process. Moreover, on Zanzibar itself Seyyid Said settled Omani planters from his Arabian state to cultivate a crop, the spice cloves, which it had been discovered grew exceptionally well there. So successful was his system that all those interested in east Africa congregated at Zanzibar: Indian traders, agents, customs farmers and capitalists advancing money for the trading caravans to the interior and for the operations of the clove estates; merchants and shippers from America, France, the Hanseatic ports (from 1871, Germany) and Britain; and the consuls of the various states anxious to protect their nationals and their commercial interests.

The British had had a close interest in Muscat and Oman since 1798 because of its importance on the Levant–Gulf route to India, which Napoleon then seemed to threaten. In 1840 they instructed their agent at Muscat, Consul Hamerton, to follow the Sultan to Zanzibar, and from that time the British vied with the other consuls to secure the main influence over the Sultan and hence over the coast. They signed a commercial treaty with Zanzibar, and British India soon came to dominate the trade of the island. Moreover, the Sultan realized that the British were the most important power in the Indian Ocean and that an alliance with them could only enhance his own power. After his death in 1856, the successors of Seyyid Said attempted from time to time to throw off the power of the British, but by the 1870s it was an impossible task.

The British used their efforts to destroy the east African slave trade to trap the Zanzibar sultans. By a series of treaties, in 1822, 1862 and 1873, they sought to cut back the slave trade of the Indian Ocean. To enforce these treaties, the British increased the Sultan's power. In reality he was only a suzerain, to whom other

24

rulers on the coast paid a relatively vague allegiance, in return for a subsidy from the Zanzibar customs revenues. To make the slave trade treaties effective, the British attempted to turn him into an executive ruler ruling an east African state encompassing not only the coastal trading towns, but also inland areas traversed by the commercial caravans from Zanzibar. Having created this artificial power, the British backed it up by the use of their naval squadron, and by organizing and arming a small modern army for the Sultan under the command of a British naval officer. But the coastal towns repeatedly attempted to reassert their independence, for the new policy was cutting at the very roots of their prosperity. Moreover, in the interior the majority of Africans lived beyond the influence of Zanzibar.

The British had in fact created a neat system of informal rule. The British naval squadron not only sought out slavers, it also protected British trade and the Indian Ocean routes to India. In 1872, a British scheduled shipping service, with a mail contract which paid a great deal more than the quantity of mail justified (a favourite imperial device to encourage the establishment of a service), was begun to Zanzibar. From 1873, the British consul-general at Zanzibar, Sir John Kirk, exercised considerable power over the Sultan, Barghash, and between 1870 and 1879 the tonnage of British shipping at Zanzibar increased sevenfold. In 1879 the submarine cable reached Zanzibar and formed a junction there for lines both to Mauritius and to South Africa. Zanzibar had now become a vital communications station on the way to other colonies, a position that the British would not give up.

However, the British efforts to protect the Sultan and his dominions were becoming more problematical. The first threat came from Egypt. In 1875, the Khedive, anxious to extend Egypt's growing power within its own region – using European officers to command its forces and its administration – decided to consolidate his hold on the upper Nile by securing a position in east Africa. A British captain in Egyptian employ annexed a small part of the east African coast for Egypt, but the British Government warned Egypt off the Sultan of Zanzibar's territory.

The British, however, declined to submit to pressures that their own direct power in east Africa should be extended. These pressures came partly from missionaries, who had followed the great explorers Krapf, Rebmann, Livingstone, Burton and Speke into east Africa. Mission stations had been founded on the coast as early as the 1840s, and by the 1860s and 1870s they were penetrating the interior. The pressures also came from commercial and shipping interests associated with Zanzibar. The shipping route to Zanzibar had been founded by a Scottish shipowner, Sir William Mackinnon, who had made a sizeable fortune from a great shipping line which connected India with all her Indian Ocean trading partners. He was closely connected with Scottish missionaries and British humanitarian circles, and seems to have wanted to use his wealth to carve out a place for himself in the annals of British imperial expansion. He established a close relationship with other members of the imperial élite in London (just as Rhodes was to do) and became involved in a variety of imperial schemes. In 1877, he attempted to found a company to 'develop' the coastal and interior dominions (dominions that were more theoretical than real) of the Sultan of Zanzibar. The Foreign Office, however, declined to give its blessing, and it was to be nearly ten years before Mackinnon's project was revived.

By that time further pressures had developed. German traders were well established in Zanzibar, and a powerful German shipping magnate also started a service there. A British botanist and explorer, Harry Johnston, had waxed enthusiastic about the opportunities for white settlement on the healthy uplands of east Africa. Two German colonization societies were founded, also with ambitions to found a colony of white settlement, in the hope that Germans might be persuaded to settle on German overseas territory rather than migrate to the United States. A German explorer, Karl Peters, the founder of the German Colonization Society, arrived in east Africa in 1884 to collect treaties. There was much wild talk about the economic potential of the region on the part of both British and German explorers, who suggested that ivory and rubber exports could support an administration, that white settlement could create a new British or German dominion, and that the more densely populated African states in the lake area, now Uganda, could become an important market for European goods.

East Africa turned out to be a great economic disappointment to European imperialism, and that has led historians to stress the non-economic aspects of the ambitions of people like Mackinnon, but we should never discount the influence of the wildly optimistic reports of economic potential that came out of east Africa. Such reports inevitably led to fears of rival expansionism. Leopold of the Belgians seemed to develop east African coastal ambitions for his great Congo territory. At the same time, the Sultanate of Zanzibar seemed a great deal less secure as an agent of British power in the region. British actions against slavery and the slave trade had cut off the Sultan from his aristocracy, who saw their economic and social position undermined. Moreover, the price of cloves collapsed, and both the Sultan and plantation owners found themselves heavily in debt to Indian traders and moneylenders.

The instability of Zanzibar and the ambitions of Leopold might well have produced change in east Africa, but again it was the arrival of the Germans which precipitated the Partition. Bismarck, aware of the growing popularity of the new imperial societies and under pressure from German shipping interests, decided to give official sanction to the concessions secured by Karl Peters and the German Colonization Society. This occurred in early 1885 in the wake of the German moves in the Cameroons, Togo and south-west Africa. Peters and his associates received a charter on the British model to conduct both commerce and administration in east Africa. At first the British attempted to protect the Sultan's dominions, but anxious not to offend Bismarck, they soon co-operated with the Germans. They agreed upon a division of east Africa into spheres of influence in 1886, and Mackinnon, encouraged by British officials, revived the concession which he had failed to have ratified ten years earlier. The British Government now received the proposal sympathetically and provided him with a charter. His company, the Imperial British East Africa Company, chartered in 1888, was given the right to develop and administer the whole of what were later to be the colonies of Kenya and Uganda. During the brief existence of the company, the impossibility of the task rapidly became apparent. The company lacked capital, and could not secure

27

Africa and the Ottoman Empire in 1914

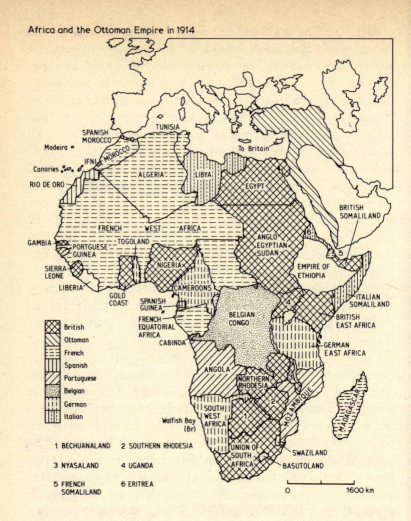

SPANISH MOROCCO
TUNISIA
Madeira
MOROCCO
IFNI
Canaries
RIO DE ORO
ALGERIA
LIBYA
To Britain
EGYPT
BRITISH SOMALILAND
FRENCH   WEST   AFRICA
GAMBIA
PORTUGUESE GUINEA
TOGOLAND
NIGERIA
ANGLO EGYPTIAN SUDAN
SIERRA LEONE
LIBERIA
GOLD COAST
EMPIRE OF ETHIOPIA
6
5
CAMEROONS
SPANISH GUINEA
FRENCH EQUATORIAL AFRICA
CABINDA
BELGIAN CONGO
4
ITALIAN SOMALILAND
BRITISH EAST AFRICA
GERMAN EAST AFRICA
ANGOLA
NORTHERN RHODESIA
3
MOZAMBIQUE
MADAGASCAR
Walfish Bay (Br)
SOUTH WEST AFRICA
1
2
UNION OF SOUTH AFRICA
SWAZILAND
BASUTOLAND

British
Ottoman
French
Spanish
Portuguese
Belgian
German
Italian

1 BECHUANALAND   2 SOUTHERN RHODESIA

3 NYASALAND   4 UGANDA

5 FRENCH   6 ERITREA
  SOMALILAND

0   1600 km

28

revenue sufficiently quickly to build the railway line which was seen as crucial. In 1894 and 1895, the British had no alternative but to declare protectorates over the territories. The Sultan, shorn of his past pretensions to east Africa, was reduced to his islands of Zanzibar and Pemba, which themselves soon became a British protectorate.

The Scramble had also reached the Horn of Africa, so strategically placed on the Suez/Red Sea/Gulf of Aden route to the East. The French and the British had each secured a position on the southern shore of the Gulf of Aden. The Italians, anxious to join the imperial club themselves, annexed Eritrea in 1885 as well as a large portion of Somaliland (also formerly seen as part of Zanzibar's coastal dominions) in 1889, though their efforts to extend their empire into one of the few remaining independent parts of Africa, Ethiopia, were checked at the Battle of Adowa in 1896. With this one exception, the partition of east Africa was complete.

Interpretation

As we have seen, the Partition was not a sudden and wholly unpremeditated affair. 'Creeping partition' had been going on in Africa for some time. The French had already conceived grand designs in the 1870s, and commercial pressures had been exerted on the British from the same period. Nevertheless, the speed with which the Partition was finally accomplished, after more than 300 years of European coastal activity, and the comprehensiveness of the land grab do suggest that this was a new and dramatic phase. Historians have elaborated and debated many different theories to explain the events of the 1880s and 1890s.

These interpretations have overlaid each other, and it is perhaps helpful to divide them into categories to bring some order to a very complex process of theorizing. It has become customary to divide explanations into metropolitan and peripheral, economic and non-economic. Metropolitan interpretations are those which seek to explain the Scramble in terms of developments in Europe, while peripheral ones look to events in Africa itself. The economic–non-economic categories cut across the metropolitan–peripheral ones, so that there are some metropolitan and some peripheral explanations which are also economic and some which are not.

(a) Capitalist imperialism

The first explanation offered for the Partition in the early years of this century saw the European grab for Africa as arising from an inherent problem in capitalism. To maintain their capacity for growth capitalist economies had repeatedly to find new outlets for investment. In the late nineteenth century, the capitalist economies entered upon a particularly difficult period. Rates of return on capital invested at home were falling, and so capitalists believed that surplus capital had to be exported. Further, this interpretation suggests that the power to dispose of capital was falling into fewer hands, particularly large banking interests. Those who disposed of such capital desired that it should be protected, and imperialism was therefore the policy of a small, highly influential capitalist group.

Certainly this was a period of considerable capital exports from Europe, and such exports played an important role in the development of Europe's relationship with the world as a whole, but this explanation seems to offer little help for the Partition of Africa. Significant amounts of capital were exported to South Africa, but Africa generally remained the continent receiving less investment than any other right up to the first world war. Moreover, the development of great capitalist combines and concentrated banking interests did not occur until after the Partition had been accomplished.

(b) Markets

The second metropolitan explanation is also economic. This suggests that European capitalist economies had encountered not so much a crisis of excess capital as a crisis of excess competition and production. Germany and the United States were industrializing rapidly, and France and Italy were also attempting to produce their industrial response. The British experience showed that industrialism necessarily involved global specialization. The industrial state had to maintain itself through an exchange of foodstuffs and raw materials for industrial goods. No industrial state could be self-sufficient, and to survive it had to export. New industrial states had to find new markets or encroach on those of existing exporters. Colonies could offer assured markets, particularly if the European state's relationship with them was protected by tariffs which would keep competitors out.

In addition, the capitalist economies seemed to have moved into a period of depression between the 1870s and 1890s. There were downturns in trading activity in the decade preceding the Scramble and again in the 1880s and 1890s when the Scramble was at its height. These difficulties caused alarm to industrialists and merchants throughout Europe. Italy, Germany and France responded with new tariffs in 1878, 1879 and 1881 respectively, and that compounded alarm in Britain, where the Government was still wedded to free trade. It is true that protectionist policies did not come fully to fruition until the 1890s, but the anxiety was there at the earlier period. Some indication of the alarm in Britain can be secured from the Royal Commission appointed to enquire into the Depression of Trade and Industry in 1885–6. Chambers of Commerce and Trades Societies, representing both employers and labour, were circularized as to the reasons for the depression, and their suggestions for the measures that could be taken to alleviate it. Many commented on foreign competition and tariffs, and several urged the opening of new markets, for example in Africa, and the consolidation of trading relations with colonies.

Again this market explanation, though much used at the time as an argument that colonial expansion should be undertaken, is limited in the African case. Africa's population was small, and the opportunities for marketing industrial goods were slight. But hopes are invariably more potent than reality.

(c) Raw materials

If markets are one end of the industrial chain, raw materials are the other. The early phase of the industrial revolution depended on iron and coal which were available in Europe, and on cotton which had to be supplied by the United States and later by India and Egypt. But by the late nineteenth century other raw materials

31

were beginning to be important. Vegetable oils were used in the manufacture of soaps and industrial lubricants. The large firm of Lever Brothers on Merseyside built its power mainly on west African palm oil, and Liverpool was the port most closely connected with the west African trade. Rubber had become important for insulation of the new electrical and telegraph wires and for tyres. Until the rubber plantations were developed in Malaya at the beginning of this century, rubber was only collected in the wild in South America and in Africa.

There was also a great boom in the manufacture of ivory goods at this time – keys for the piano industry which experienced huge growth in the late nineteenth century, handles for the cutlery industry, billiard balls for an indoor sport now much in vogue. So great was the demand for ivory that prices remained high (as did rubber prices) throughout the 'depression' when the prices of many other commodities fell. Another new taste developing in Europe was the burgeoning demand for chocolate. Cocoa was grown on Spanish and Portuguese offshore islands in west Africa. In 1879 it was introduced to the Gold Coast (Ghana) and within twenty years it had transformed the economy of the region. Important companies like Cadbury and Rowntree became closely bound up with the west African trade in cocoa. This cocoa transfer was made by an African, but such botanical experimentation in continental transfer of foodstuffs and agricultural raw materials was regarded as one of the scientific achievements of the age. Several explorers were keen botanists and travelled with an eye to the establishment of plantation crops. Natural fibres and many other commodities would be important in the next phase of industrial development.

It was recognized too that the new industrial age would emphasize base metals like copper. Copper deposits were well known in Africa, for Africans had exploited them for hundreds of years, and in many places had used copper as a currency. If base metals were to become more important, gold retained the fascination it had held for Europeans for many centuries. All industrial states had placed their currencies on the gold standard in the nineteenth century in order to stabilize them, and were building up reserves of gold to underpin these currencies. Gold had therefore become, even more than before, a source of power and stability for the western economic system. Some of the older sources of gold were beginning to decline in significance, so no state could allow a vital source of gold like the Transvaal to fall into the hands of a protectionist rival.

There was, therefore, much discussion of Africa as a source of raw materials, and the continent was likely to be more significant as a supplier than as a market. But raw materials had been extracted from Africa for many years without the need for political controls. The mere existence of raw materials does not fully explain why Europe felt it necessary to partition the continent, although there can be no doubt that the pace was quickening, and the fears and hopes were intensifying at this period.

(d)   Statesmen's imperialism

This political and diplomatic explanation sees the Partition as part of European statesmen's power-play. Statesmen used overseas territories as bargaining counters in a global game of diplomacy, as a safety valve for European nationalist tensions. This idea has always been suggested most forcibly with reference to Bismarck, who has been seen by some as actually precipitating the Scramble in order to secure his diplomatic ends in Europe, namely the isolation of France. It is a view which is no longer fashionable, for it smacks too much of the influence of 'great men' upon history, and the forces at work in Africa were much too powerful and complex to be controlled or manipulated by single political figures. Even before Leopold and Bismarck took a hand, some form of Partition was gathering momentum.

However, the last acts of the Partition in north Africa do seem to have rather more diplomatic content. Britain had the most considerable economic interests in Morocco, but she allowed France to have a free run there. Even so France did not declare a protectorate over Morocco (partitioning it with Spain) until threatened by Germany in the Moroccan crises of 1905 and 1911.

(e)   Imperialism and nationalism

This is the argument that the Partition of Africa occurred as a by-product of the friction created by new aggressive nationalisms in

33

Europe rubbing against old-established centralized states and imperial powers. Both Germany and Italy were newly united states in this period. Both had to satisfy strongly nationalist demands within them; both sought to use colonial policies to reconcile internal tensions. Italy was already dreaming of re-creating the Roman empire in the 1870s and turned her attention to Tunis, the historic Carthage. Both Germany and Italy made grabs for territory in 1884 and 1885. Neither seemed to base its claim on strong existing commercial rights. In both countries there were powerful colonial propaganda groups at work looking to empire as a means whereby the new nation states could come of age. Moreover in Germany, with its liberal franchise, a colonial policy seemed to be a popular one. It has even been said that Bismarck staged his colonial advances on several fronts in 1884 as an electioneering stunt for the election that took place in Germany late that year.

If Germany and Italy represented the aggressive force of new nationalisms, Britain and France represented the defensiveness of the old. For France after all, the German empire had been proclaimed in the aftermath of the humiliation of the Franco-Prussian War of 1870–1, in which France lost Alsace-Lorraine. A forward French policy dated from the 1870s. Defeat forced France to look outwards. Colonies, it has been suggested, were a balm for French wounded pride. The British on the other hand had been accustomed to secure their commercial ends without competition from other powers. Sometimes they had been forced to annex territory in the mid-nineteenth century, but generally they had avoided it. The British had preferred to work through informal empire, and British politicians were reluctant to translate that into formal control unless some very important national interest demanded it. From 1880 the British were forced to do so repeatedly to protect their interests from the new aggressive nationalisms and the revived imperial vision of France.

(f) Popular imperialism

It has also been argued that the new nationalisms were not just a matter for statesmen and colonial pressure groups; they also satisfied popular psychological needs. European peoples (and no

34

state was immune from this) developed an aggressive xenophobia in order to define sharply their national identity and national ambition. In Britain this came to be known as jingoism, a term significantly coined from a music-hall song at the time of the Congress of Berlin of 1878, an international conference which had an important bearing on the Partition. Popular culture, as expressed in the theatre and popular songs, took on a strongly nationalist and patriotic tone, and this inevitably became bound up with at least the protection, if not the extension of empire. Indeed, it became a great age of propaganda. The expansion of education led to a considerable increase in literacy, and this was exploited by colonial pressure groups, the army, the navy and above all the missions.

The missions were very important in propagating imperial ideas. Mission societies, which had appeared in all denominations and in all European countries in the nineteenth century, became convinced of their divine mission to convert the world, to save other people from what they saw to be 'barbarism' and 'savagery'. To achieve this, they required both money and recruits, and they set about opening people's pockets and minds through every publicity technique available to them. Notable missionaries became heroes, and books by them or about them became best-sellers. These and other popular works propagated racial ideas which seemed at one and the same time both to explain and to justify European technical and military superiority in the world.

It has sometimes been objected that 'popular imperialism' was a result of the Partition and other imperial advances of the age, not a cause. But popular imperialism does seem to have its roots in the 1870s and imperial events did raise popular outcries. Good examples are the Congress of Berlin in 1878, the death of General Gordon in 1885, the proposal to hand over the missions of southern Nyasaland to the Portuguese in 1890, the possibility of abandoning Uganda in 1893–4, Fashoda, 1898, and above all during the Boer War, 1899–1902. Thus popular opinion certainly seems to have been significant by the 1890s when politicians were confirming the more tentative moves (the chartering of companies, for example) of the 1880s. These are all

British examples, but 'jingoism' was just as evident in the rest of Europe.

Electoral behaviour is of course the best index of popular opinion. We have already seen that Bismarck may well have been responding to electoral pressures in 1884. In Britain, there can be no doubt that colonial discontents contributed to the fall of Gladstone in 1885, and when he formed his fourth ministry in 1892 the Liberal Party had developed a strongly imperialist complexion. His successor, Rosebery, was almost indistinguishable from any Conservative imperialist. Even the Labour movement had imperial elements within it: some Labour leaders accepted the idea that the possession of empire was important to the interests of the working classes, or that it was an inevitable obligation which had to be fulfilled in as ethical a manner as was possible. To attack the possession of colonies seemed to be unpatriotic, and therefore electorally dangerous.

(g) Feudal atavism

Another social explanation is one that sees imperialism as the policy of the surviving feudal elements of European society, military castes which sought new employment and the continuation of their influence. In France, imperial attitudes were largely forged in the military establishments of Algeria. Both the German and Italian empires had a strongly military flavour, administrators being usually military men rather than civilians. Empire provided them with a source of power removed from domestic politics. Even in the British empire, where the principle of civilian rule was firmly established, the army found an opportunity for employment, and an excuse for growth. In all the empires, colonial revenues could be used to pay for a proportion of the army, a technique long used by the British in India.

(h) Technology

Another explanation, at least for the timing of the Partition, is one which highlights the importance of technology. This suggests that railways, steamships, the telegraph, and medical advances were crucial to the Partition, which could not have been achieved without them.

36

By the 1870s, railways had become a sort of imperial panacea. They could bind together the Canadian Confederation after 1867; perhaps they could achieve similar feats in Australasia and southern Africa; they could open up vast tracts of the world to trade and settlement. The French developed a penchant for grandiose railway schemes in the 1870s and 1880s, and saw them as a central feature of imperial acquisition. For the British too, proposals to extend territory invariably carried with them some plan of railway building which it was thought would make the new territory viable. Both the Imperial British East Africa Company and the British South Africa Company thought of railways as an essential part of their plans for development. Rhodes's inflated ideas would have been more difficult to achieve but for the great extension of the Cape railway system which had occurred in the previous decade.

But it was technical developments in steamships which were perhaps most important in this period. Until the 1870s, marine engines were extremely inefficient in that they had to carry so much fuel that there was space for little else. Marine engine technology was revolutionized by the invention of the triple-expansion engine, which made much more efficient use of steam. With the growth of liner services (that is ships following published regular schedules) to west Africa, south Africa and east Africa, shipping interests became a powerful pressure group anxious for the extension of trade and the protection of important harbours. Both in Britain and in Germany shipping magnates were closely bound up with imperial expansion.

Perhaps the most remarkable contribution of the steamship was its appearance on the rivers and lakes of Africa. Hundreds of small steam vessels appeared on rivers like the Niger, the Congo, the Zambezi and the Shiré in the years before the Partition. Rapids were circumvented by the simple expedient of constructing vessels up-river and running them on the long stretches between cataracts. Similarly, steamers were carried overland in sections and rebuilt on the shores of the great lakes of east Africa. Both missionaries and traders were in this way given access to hundreds of miles of coastline around, for example, Lakes Tanganyika and Malawi. The success of lake and river steamers in the years before the Scramble emphasized the importance of water communications and made rivers and lakes the vital plums for the scrambling powers.

The third technical obsession of the age was the telegraph, particularly the undersea cable. The telegraph arrived in south and east Africa in 1879, and in west Africa in 1885. Commercial and military requirements, administrative decisions and news could now be sent in a matter of hours, instead of weeks and months as in the past. Ships, goods and troops could rapidly be sent where required.

But some would say that the most important technical advance of all was in armaments. By the 1860s and 1870s vast numbers of guns had come to circulate in Africa. Many of these were ancient muskets, for Europeans often unloaded obsolete stock on to Africa. Guns were the main exchange item for ivory, and in southern Africa Africans went to work for Europeans in order to acquire them. By the time of the Scramble Africans were acquiring more modern rifles and breech-loading weapons. In 1889 the planners of the British South Africa Company offered Lobengula, King of the Ndebele in Zimbabwe, 1000 of the very latest Martini-Henry rifles to persuade him to give them the concession they desired. But Europeans had by now established a tremendous technological gap in firearms. Fast-repeating machine guns had been invented (the gatling in the late 1860s and the maxim soon after), and these enabled Europeans to conquer large African armies with small forces. Europeans took care never to supply Africans with machine guns.

If Europeans had at last become a military match for Africans, they were also solving some of the medical problems of Africa. From the 1850s, quinine was being used as a prophylactic (that is a medicine taken to prevent the outbreak of disease rather than cure it after it had occurred) and efforts were being made to overcome the difficulties of the tsetse fly. Europeans now carried a range of patent medicines, water purifiers and the iike. Death rates declined dramatically in this period, and west Africa in particular ceased to be the 'white man's grave' it had been in an earlier age.

Clearly, such technical advances did not create imperialism in Africa, but they did produce the vital conditions that rendered its extension more readily possible. Moreover, such technical achievements seemed to emphasize the cultural gap between Europe and Africa which was important in the popular thinking of the period.

PERIPHERAL

(i) Strategic and Egyptocentric

Perhaps the first and most influential peripheral explanation is that which relates the entire Partition to the crisis in Egypt and the two routes to India. As we have seen, the British invaded Egypt in 1882. The French, having apparently lost their former influence in Egypt, now looked for compensation elsewhere and this provoked Anglo-French rivalries in west Africa.

The vital point about this interpretation is that the British went into Egypt not to protect the bondholders, but for strategic reasons, to protect the Suez Canal and the crucial route to India. Similarly, British interest in the Cape was strategic, to protect the Cape route to the East and the important Royal Navy base at Simon's Bay. The British could not permit any other power to achieve an interior preponderance which might threaten the Cape, and it was this that drew them into the interior. The Partition in east Africa was bound up with the strategic concern with the Nile. The British believed that their position in Egypt was only secure if they commanded the entire Nile system. To keep the French from the upper Nile they needed a convenient route from the east coast. It was this consideration that lay behind the retention of Uganda and the decision to build the east African railway. According to this view, the Partition of Africa is no more than a giant footnote to the British Indian empire. This interpretation had great influence for some time, but it can now be discounted. French advances were not necessarily related to Egypt. The complex interaction of peripheral and metropolitan forces, for example in south Africa, renders such a single-cause interpretation untenable.

(j) Peripheral crises

However, the importance of interpretation (i) was that it focused attention on the periphery. The result was the appearance of an

39

extensive multi-causal rather than mono-causal explanation. European penetration of Africa took a variety of different forms, debt-financing and concession-seeking in the north, trade in the west, settlement in the south and trade and strategy in the east. In west Africa, falling commodity prices squeezed the profits of European merchants, and caused them to be discontented with the old system of working through African middlemen. In southern Africa, creeping white advance and dramatic disruptions to African society repeatedly destabilized the frontier. In some places the peripheral crisis took the form of a 'crisis of collaboration'. Europeans had entered a whole series of economic relationships with Arab and African people and to facilitate these arrangements they collaborated with certain sectors of indigenous society, invariably a ruling élite. This eventually provoked resistance from those whose position was damaged by the collaborationist system. Resistance could take the form of anti-foreign outbursts, rioting and killing of Europeans, or attempted *coups d'état*. At this point, European governments intervened to resolve the crises by imposing direct imperial rule. Egypt and Zanzibar both offer examples of this sequence of events, although in the Zanzibar case the main anti-foreign outburst came after the Partition was well advanced.

(k) Sub-imperialism

Yet another peripheral interpretation sees the partition as arising from a series of sub-imperialisms. It was not so much the metropolitan powers which stimulated imperial expansion as their agents overseas. These agents were often 'colonials', settlers in existing colonies of settlement who were anxious about their own frontiers or economic opportunities. They could also be local administrators who faced particular problems of security and revenue-raising in their territories. These peripheral Europeans, settlers and 'men on the spot' cajoled and eventually convinced their mother governments to extend imperial rule. Thus, one of the origins of the partition of the world lies in the Australian colonists' desire to secure the Pacific islands against foreign encroachment in the 1870s (the threat largely came from Germany). In the case of Africa, Algeria constituted an important source of sub-imperialism for the French. Algerian settlers and military administrators were always anxious about their western, eastern and southern frontiers, as well as hoping for great trading connections southwards. In the case of the British empire, the Indian Government was more concerned with expansion in the Indian Ocean and elsewhere in the East than the Government in London was. Nevertheless, the consulate-general in Zanzibar was transferred from the Indian Government to the Foreign Office at the crucial moment in the 1870s. Perhaps the outstanding example of sub-imperialism was the activities of the settlers in southern Africa. The partition of south and central Africa was not so much a metropolitan matter as a classic instance of peripheral sub-imperialism dragging the metropolitan power after it. Still, the vital decisions to issue charters, declare protectorates or effect annexations had to be made by the parent power. The French Government often had a more grandiose vision of imperial conquest than its 'colonials' did, although that vision was usually created by imperial officials securing power in the central government.

(l) African participation

So far all these explanations have placed most of the initiatives with Europeans. But more recent historical writing has set out to demonstrate that Africans were not merely passive spectators of these events. They also took initiatives: they made treaties; they attempted to play off one European claimant against another; sometimes they collaborated, often they resisted. Some actually demanded protection – particularly in southern Africa – in order to ward off their enemies. So successful were some African diplomats in sending their representatives to London, arousing missionary and humanitarian support, that their activities have been described as a 'scramble for protection'. This African activity certainly influenced the pattern of the Partition, but it obviously cannot be used to explain the great push that the Scramble represented.

(m) The general crisis

Finally, there is an interpretation which we can perhaps describe as 'global'. It seems to combine aspects of several of the interpretations listed above, notably *(b)*, *(c)*, *(h)*, *(j)*, and *(k)*. This suggests that there was a 'general crisis' in the relations between European and non-European peoples at this time, a general crisis induced by the European efforts to create a fully integrated world economy. Industrial Europe required a highly specialized world, in which some areas would produce food for its industrial proletariat, others would produce raw materials for the industrial process, and the entire world would constitute a market for industrial goods. But to achieve this Europe needed to recast the world in its own image, to create the same infrastructures and similar institutions that would permit resources to be exploited and trade to be conducted. By the end of the nineteenth century it was apparent that Europe required a greater degree of coercion to press forward this process, coercion that could only be effected by direct imperial rule. In some areas people were resisting the new dispensation, and in consequence new military and political techniques were required to supplement the purely economic relationship.

This explanation is attractive because it appears to subsume metropolitan and peripheral elements, social and military strains, the widening of the technological gap, and the heightened tensions of the period under one umbrella thesis associated with a particular stage of economic development in the world. But there are some problems with it too. There were crises in some areas of the world, notably China, Siam, Persia and the Gulf, which did not lead to the imposition of direct political controls. But even more significantly from our point of view, there were large areas of Africa, on the face of it much less important economically than the Asian regions just mentioned, where no immediate crisis seemed to have occurred, and yet where political controls were established.

CONCLUSION

We must now attempt to draw from this complex set of explanations some answers to the question posed at the beginning of the pamphlet. Why did the European powers cease their long-standing process of nibbling at Africa and suddenly seize huge chunks of the continent?

There are a number of theses that we can reject straightaway. It seems to have had little to do with the export of capital. The 'great man' explanation simply will not do, for statesmen were largely reacting to the growing pressures and a climate of opinion which they found difficult to oppose. Napoleon III may have had ambitions in the 1850s; Leopold II had personal pretensions by the 1870s; individual Germans like Nachtigal and Peters hoped that Germany would institute an imperial policy; Mackinnon, Goldie and Rhodes all developed, to varying degrees, a passionate interest in the extension of British rule. But none of these was able to achieve his ambitions until the necessary forces came together. Finally, the Egyptocentric and strategic thesis is no longer convincing except as a powerful expression of one motivation of one European country. French decisions to advance in west Africa were made ahead of the British invasion of Egypt. French and Italian rivalries in north Africa, for example over Tunisia, and new German ambitions cannot be related to it. And in southern Africa developments were much too complex to be linked solely to the route to India.

Other 'explanations' are not really explanations at all. Public opinion, technology and African initiatives cannot explain the Partition, but they can demonstrate that the convergence of forces was now such that a partition was more likely to take place. Indeed, one of the remarkable things about the 1870s and 1880s was that so many developments in the realm of ideas, in missionary activity, in propaganda, in the technical and military gap between Europe and the rest of the world did seem to converge. A set of background conditions made the partition much easier to accomplish.

Why then were the crucial decisions made against the background of these conditions? One thing does now seem to be clear, and that is that we cannot be satisfied with an explanation which is wholly European or solely peripheral. Very important lines of force were developed from the periphery, but the thinking of people in Europe was also vital. Despite the creeping imperialism of the British and the French in west Africa, or the creeping partition of southern Africa by Dutch and English settlers, wholesale extensions of territory were resisted for a time. Both Goldie and

Mackinnon had their pleas for a recognition of their concessions and the provision of charters rejected at first. Yet a few years later they were accepted. This is not to say that they simply went into cold storage until statesmen decided to use them. It is to say that the tensions, anxieties and pressures had not yet reached the necessary pitch. If there was a convergence of background conditions, there also had to be a conjunction of economic, social and political tensions between metropolis and periphery.

The Scramble for Africa seems to have emerged from a combination of exaggerated hope and over-heated anxiety. The economic conditions of the day, the trough between the first industrial revolution of coal, cotton and iron, and the second of electricity, copper, steel; the appearance of new industrial states protecting themselves with tariffs; the decline in some commodity prices; and the heightened commercial competition everywhere produced all the alarms associated with the transition from one economic system to another. At the same time there were many publicists concerned to argue that Africa was a tropical treasure house, capable of producing plantation crops, base and precious metals, as well as other valuable commodities like rubber and ivory. Verney Lovett Cameron, who had been sent to find Livingstone, published just such an ecstatic account in his *Across Africa* in 1877. Many others wrote in similar vein. The growth in the palm oil trade, the buoyant prices of rubber and ivory, the discovery of diamonds and then of gold, all seemed to confirm this view. Africa could solve some of the problems of the age. A state which missed out on these opportunities might be imperilled in the future. These hopes and anxieties took some time to foment fully, but by the mid-1880s they were ready to blow the lid off the politicians' restraint. Politicians do not so much act as react to the forces round about them.

An influential generation was seized by this combination of exaggerated fear and overpowering ambition. Although it is difficult to see a small group of finance capitalists influencing governments to do their bidding, there was nevertheless a rather more extensive and powerful élite at work. In London, Paris and Berlin, commercial, shipping, geographical, intellectual and official figures did come together to press for imperial advance.

44

Although politicians, particularly in Britain, liked to claim that no official actions were taken to further the interests of individual investors and economic concerns, in fact they were. The London élite was closely connected by ties of education, social life and marriage. Some officials in the Foreign and Colonial Offices developed close connections with capitalist concerns and furthered their ends from a growing conviction of the need for British expansion. Ex-ministers joined the boards of companies, and colonial administrators were often rewarded with directorships of companies whose ends they had furthered when in office. This was not a conspiracy; it was merely the normal operations of such an élite group converted to a dominant idea.

There was, moreover, something irrational about the Partition – as reflected in the grandiose ambitions of figures like Leopold, Rhodes, Peters, even Mackinnon – which deeply disturbed the rational minds of politicians like Salisbury and Bismarck. In many respects the Scramble was not so much a reaction to events that had already taken place as to events that it was feared might take place. It was less the result of a 'general crisis' than a symptom of the anxieties that a general crisis was on the way.

There was much that was chimerical about the Partition, and in many parts of Africa it produced disappointing results. South Africa remained the world's most important source of gold, yet by 1910 the British had abdicated political control there. Central Africa was to be one of the western world's most important sources of copper, but this was not fully exploited until the years before the second world war. In some places European coercion upon Africans to produce agricultural raw materials or to go out to work produced large-scale revolts. Railway lines often failed to pay, and administrations invariably required subsidies from the mother countries. Some of the resources of Africa, such as the oil of Nigeria, were scarcely even discovered during the imperial period.

In retrospect, Keltie's opening sentence takes on a new significance. Not only was the speed of Europe's grab for Africa a most remarkable episode, so was the speed of Europe's withdrawal. Many Africans were born before the Partition occurred, and were still alive when Europe departed in the early 1960s. By that time

Africa had perhaps been recast in Europe's image, with recognizable national boundaries, an infrastructure of sorts, and relatively similar institutions. But was that what the original Scramblers really intended?

Bibliography

The literature on the Partition is exceptionally extensive. Listed below are some basic works which contain longer bibliographies

General

Chamberlain, M. E. (1974) *The Scramble for Africa*, London – contains some useful documents.

Economic background

Cain, P. J. (1980) *Economic Foundations of British Overseas Expansion*, London.

Forbes Munro, J. (1976) *Africa and the International Economy*, London.

Hodgart, Alan (1977) *The Economics of European Imperialism*, London.

Interpretations

Brunschwig, H. (1966) *French Colonialism, 1871–1914*, London – political.

Fieldhouse, D. K. (1967) *The Theory of Capitalist Imperialism*, London – readings on the export of capital.

Fieldhouse, D. K. (1973) *Economics and Empire, 1830–1914*, London – peripheral multi-causal.

Galbraith, John S. (1972) *Mackinnon and East Africa*, Cambridge – peripheral–metropolitan, non-economic.

Hargreaves, J. D. (1963) *Prelude to the Partition of West Africa*, London.

————— (1974) *West Africa Partitioned* (vol. 1), London – peripheral Anglo-French rivalries.

Headrick, D. R. (1981) *The Tools of Empire*, Oxford – technology and European imperialism.

Hynes, William G. (1979) *The Economics of Empire, Britain, Africa, and the New Imperialism*, London – commercial pressures and the slumps of the 1880s and 1890s.

Robinson, R. and Gallagher, J. (1961) *Africa and the Victorians*, London – peripheral, strategic, Egyptocentric.

Schreuder, D. M. (1980) *The Scramble for Southern Africa*, Cambridge – peripheral sub-imperialism.

NOTES

NOTES

NOTES